TRAINSPOTTER'S NOTEBOOK

TO RECORD THE TRAINS YOU SEE

DEDICATION

To the committed spotters

This notebook is for all those who love the thrill of the chase down the platform – whatever the weather.

THIS NOTEBOOK BELONGS TO:

_____

_____

ACKNOWLEDGMENTS

To my son, who taught me to love trains
as much as he does.

DATE:
TIME:
TRAIN:
HEADCODE:
OPERATING COMPANY:
COMING FROM:
GOING TO:
OTHER INFORMATION:

DATE:
TIME:
TRAIN:
HEADCODE:
OPERATING COMPANY:
COMING FROM:
GOING TO:
OTHER INFORMATION:

DATE:
TIME:
TRAIN:
HEADCODE:
OPERATING COMPANY:
COMING FROM:
GOING TO:
OTHER INFORMATION:

| DATE: |
| TIME: |
| TRAIN: |
| |
| HEADCODE: |
| OPERATING COMPANY: |
| |
| COMING FROM: |
| |
| GOING TO: |
| |
| OTHER INFORMATION: |
| |
| |
| |
| |
| |
| |
| |
| |
| |

DATE:
TIME:
TRAIN:
HEADCODE:
OPERATING COMPANY:
COMING FROM:
GOING TO:
OTHER INFORMATION:

DATE:
TIME:
TRAIN:
HEADCODE:
OPERATING COMPANY:
COMING FROM:
GOING TO:
OTHER INFORMATION:

DATE:
TIME:
TRAIN:
HEADCODE:
OPERATING COMPANY:
COMING FROM:
GOING TO:
OTHER INFORMATION:

DATE:
TIME:
TRAIN:
HEADCODE:
OPERATING COMPANY:
COMING FROM:
GOING TO:
OTHER INFORMATION:

DATE:
TIME:
TRAIN:
HEADCODE:
OPERATING COMPANY:
COMING FROM:
GOING TO:
OTHER INFORMATION:

DATE:
TIME:
TRAIN:
HEADCODE:
OPERATING COMPANY:
COMING FROM:
GOING TO:
OTHER INFORMATION:

DATE:
TIME:
TRAIN:
HEADCODE:
OPERATING COMPANY:
COMING FROM:
GOING TO:
OTHER INFORMATION:

DATE:
TIME:
TRAIN:
HEADCODE:
OPERATING COMPANY:
COMING FROM:
GOING TO:
OTHER INFORMATION:

| DATE: |
| TIME: |
| TRAIN: |
| |
| HEADCODE: |
| OPERATING COMPANY: |
| |
| COMING FROM: |
| |
| GOING TO: |
| |
| OTHER INFORMATION: |
| |
| |
| |
| |
| |
| |
| |
| |
| |
| |

DATE:
TIME:
TRAIN:
HEADCODE:
OPERATING COMPANY:
COMING FROM:
GOING TO:
OTHER INFORMATION:

DATE:
TIME:
TRAIN:
HEADCODE:
OPERATING COMPANY:
COMING FROM:
GOING TO:
OTHER INFORMATION:

DATE:
TIME:
TRAIN:
HEADCODE:
OPERATING COMPANY:
COMING FROM:
GOING TO:
OTHER INFORMATION:

DATE:
TIME:
TRAIN:
HEADCODE:
OPERATING COMPANY:
COMING FROM:
GOING TO:
OTHER INFORMATION:

DATE:
TIME:
TRAIN:
HEADCODE:
OPERATING COMPANY:
COMING FROM:
GOING TO:
OTHER INFORMATION:

DATE:
TIME:
TRAIN:
HEADCODE:
OPERATING COMPANY:
COMING FROM:
GOING TO:
OTHER INFORMATION:

DATE:
TIME:
TRAIN:
HEADCODE:
OPERATING COMPANY:
COMING FROM:
GOING TO:
OTHER INFORMATION:

DATE:
TIME:
TRAIN:
HEADCODE:
OPERATING COMPANY:
COMING FROM:
GOING TO:
OTHER INFORMATION:

DATE:
TIME:
TRAIN:
HEADCODE:
OPERATING COMPANY:
COMING FROM:
GOING TO:
OTHER INFORMATION:

DATE:
TIME:
TRAIN:
HEADCODE:
OPERATING COMPANY:
COMING FROM:
GOING TO:
OTHER INFORMATION:

DATE:
TIME:
TRAIN:
HEADCODE:
OPERATING COMPANY:
COMING FROM:
GOING TO:
OTHER INFORMATION:

DATE:
TIME:
TRAIN:
HEADCODE:
OPERATING COMPANY:
COMING FROM:
GOING TO:
OTHER INFORMATION:

DATE:
TIME:
TRAIN:
HEADCODE:
OPERATING COMPANY:
COMING FROM:
GOING TO:
OTHER INFORMATION:

| DATE: |
| TIME: |
| TRAIN: |
| |
| HEADCODE: |
| OPERATING COMPANY: |
| |
| COMING FROM: |
| |
| GOING TO: |
| |
| OTHER INFORMATION: |
| |
| |
| |
| |
| |
| |
| |
| |
| |
| |

DATE:
TIME:
TRAIN:
HEADCODE:
OPERATING COMPANY:
COMING FROM:
GOING TO:
OTHER INFORMATION:

DATE:
TIME:
TRAIN:
HEADCODE:
OPERATING COMPANY:
COMING FROM:
GOING TO:
OTHER INFORMATION:

| DATE: |
| TIME: |
| TRAIN: |
| |
| HEADCODE: |
| OPERATING COMPANY: |
| |
| COMING FROM: |
| |
| GOING TO: |
| |
| OTHER INFORMATION: |
| |
| |
| |
| |
| |
| |
| |
| |
| |
| |

DATE:
TIME:
TRAIN:
HEADCODE:
OPERATING COMPANY:
COMING FROM:
GOING TO:
OTHER INFORMATION:

DATE:
TIME:
TRAIN:
HEADCODE:
OPERATING COMPANY:
COMING FROM:
GOING TO:
OTHER INFORMATION:

DATE:
TIME:
TRAIN:
HEADCODE:
OPERATING COMPANY:
COMING FROM:
GOING TO:
OTHER INFORMATION:

DATE:
TIME:
TRAIN:
HEADCODE:
OPERATING COMPANY:
COMING FROM:
GOING TO:
OTHER INFORMATION:

DATE:
TIME:
TRAIN:
HEADCODE:
OPERATING COMPANY:
COMING FROM:
GOING TO:
OTHER INFORMATION:

DATE:
TIME:
TRAIN:
HEADCODE:
OPERATING COMPANY:
COMING FROM:
GOING TO:
OTHER INFORMATION:

DATE:
TIME:
TRAIN:
HEADCODE:
OPERATING COMPANY:
COMING FROM:
GOING TO:
OTHER INFORMATION:

DATE:
TIME:
TRAIN:
HEADCODE:
OPERATING COMPANY:
COMING FROM:
GOING TO:
OTHER INFORMATION:

DATE:
TIME:
TRAIN:
HEADCODE:
OPERATING COMPANY:
COMING FROM:
GOING TO:
OTHER INFORMATION:

DATE:
TIME:
TRAIN:
HEADCODE:
OPERATING COMPANY:
COMING FROM:
GOING TO:
OTHER INFORMATION:

DATE:
TIME:
TRAIN:
HEADCODE:
OPERATING COMPANY:
COMING FROM:
GOING TO:
OTHER INFORMATION:

DATE:
TIME:
TRAIN:
HEADCODE:
OPERATING COMPANY:
COMING FROM:
GOING TO:
OTHER INFORMATION:

DATE:
TIME:
TRAIN:
HEADCODE:
OPERATING COMPANY:
COMING FROM:
GOING TO:
OTHER INFORMATION:

DATE:
TIME:
TRAIN:
HEADCODE:
OPERATING COMPANY:
COMING FROM:
GOING TO:
OTHER INFORMATION:

DATE:
TIME:
TRAIN:
HEADCODE:
OPERATING COMPANY:
COMING FROM:
GOING TO:
OTHER INFORMATION:

DATE:
TIME:
TRAIN:
HEADCODE:
OPERATING COMPANY:
COMING FROM:
GOING TO:
OTHER INFORMATION:

| DATE: |
| TIME: |
| TRAIN: |
| |
| HEADCODE: |
| OPERATING COMPANY: |
| |
| COMING FROM: |
| |
| GOING TO: |
| |
| OTHER INFORMATION: |
| |
| |
| |
| |
| |
| |
| |
| |
| |
| |

DATE:
TIME:
TRAIN:
HEADCODE:
OPERATING COMPANY:
COMING FROM:
GOING TO:
OTHER INFORMATION:

DATE:
TIME:
TRAIN:
HEADCODE:
OPERATING COMPANY:
COMING FROM:
GOING TO:
OTHER INFORMATION:

DATE:
TIME:
TRAIN:
HEADCODE:
OPERATING COMPANY:
COMING FROM:
GOING TO:
OTHER INFORMATION:

DATE:
TIME:
TRAIN:
HEADCODE:
OPERATING COMPANY:
COMING FROM:
GOING TO:
OTHER INFORMATION:

DATE:
TIME:
TRAIN:
HEADCODE:
OPERATING COMPANY:
COMING FROM:
GOING TO:
OTHER INFORMATION:

DATE:
TIME:
TRAIN:
HEADCODE:
OPERATING COMPANY:
COMING FROM:
GOING TO:
OTHER INFORMATION:

| DATE: |
| TIME: |
| TRAIN: |
| |
| HEADCODE: |
| OPERATING COMPANY: |
| |
| COMING FROM: |
| |
| GOING TO: |
| |
| OTHER INFORMATION: |
| |
| |
| |
| |
| |
| |
| |
| |
| |

DATE:
TIME:
TRAIN:
HEADCODE:
OPERATING COMPANY:
COMING FROM:
GOING TO:
OTHER INFORMATION:

DATE:
TIME:
TRAIN:
HEADCODE:
OPERATING COMPANY:
COMING FROM:
GOING TO:
OTHER INFORMATION:

DATE:
TIME:
TRAIN:
HEADCODE:
OPERATING COMPANY:
COMING FROM:
GOING TO:
OTHER INFORMATION:

DATE:
TIME:
TRAIN:
HEADCODE:
OPERATING COMPANY:
COMING FROM:
GOING TO:
OTHER INFORMATION:

DATE:
TIME:
TRAIN:
HEADCODE:
OPERATING COMPANY:
COMING FROM:
GOING TO:
OTHER INFORMATION:

DATE:
TIME:
TRAIN:
HEADCODE:
OPERATING COMPANY:
COMING FROM:
GOING TO:
OTHER INFORMATION:

DATE:
TIME:
TRAIN:
HEADCODE:
OPERATING COMPANY:
COMING FROM:
GOING TO:
OTHER INFORMATION:

Date:
Time:
Train:
Headcode:
Operating company:
Coming from:
Going to:
Other information:

DATE:
TIME:
TRAIN:
HEADCODE:
OPERATING COMPANY:
COMING FROM:
GOING TO:
OTHER INFORMATION:

DATE:
TIME:
TRAIN:
HEADCODE:
OPERATING COMPANY:
COMING FROM:
GOING TO:
OTHER INFORMATION:

DATE:
TIME:
TRAIN:
HEADCODE:
OPERATING COMPANY:
COMING FROM:
GOING TO:
OTHER INFORMATION:

DATE:
TIME:
TRAIN:
HEADCODE:
OPERATING COMPANY:
COMING FROM:
GOING TO:
OTHER INFORMATION:

DATE:
TIME:
TRAIN:
HEADCODE:
OPERATING COMPANY:
COMING FROM:
GOING TO:
OTHER INFORMATION:

| DATE: |
| TIME: |
| TRAIN: |
| |
| HEADCODE: |
| OPERATING COMPANY: |
| |
| COMING FROM: |
| |
| GOING TO: |
| |
| OTHER INFORMATION: |
| |
| |
| |
| |
| |
| |
| |
| |
| |
| |

DATE:
TIME:
TRAIN:
HEADCODE:
OPERATING COMPANY:
COMING FROM:
GOING TO:
OTHER INFORMATION:

DATE:
TIME:
TRAIN:
HEADCODE:
OPERATING COMPANY:
COMING FROM:
GOING TO:
OTHER INFORMATION:

DATE:
TIME:
TRAIN:
HEADCODE:
OPERATING COMPANY:
COMING FROM:
GOING TO:
OTHER INFORMATION:

DATE:
TIME:
TRAIN:
HEADCODE:
OPERATING COMPANY:
COMING FROM:
GOING TO:
OTHER INFORMATION:

DATE:
TIME:
TRAIN:
HEADCODE:
OPERATING COMPANY:
COMING FROM:
GOING TO:
OTHER INFORMATION:

DATE:
TIME:
TRAIN:
HEADCODE:
OPERATING COMPANY:
COMING FROM:
GOING TO:
OTHER INFORMATION:

DATE:
TIME:
TRAIN:
HEADCODE:
OPERATING COMPANY:
COMING FROM:
GOING TO:
OTHER INFORMATION:

DATE:
TIME:
TRAIN:
HEADCODE:
OPERATING COMPANY:
COMING FROM:
GOING TO:
OTHER INFORMATION:

DATE:
TIME:
TRAIN:
HEADCODE:
OPERATING COMPANY:
COMING FROM:
GOING TO:
OTHER INFORMATION:

DATE:
TIME:
TRAIN:
HEADCODE:
OPERATING COMPANY:
COMING FROM:
GOING TO:
OTHER INFORMATION:

DATE:
TIME:
TRAIN:
HEADCODE:
OPERATING COMPANY:
COMING FROM:
GOING TO:
OTHER INFORMATION:

DATE:
TIME:
TRAIN:
HEADCODE:
OPERATING COMPANY:
COMING FROM:
GOING TO:
OTHER INFORMATION:

DATE:
TIME:
TRAIN:
HEADCODE:
OPERATING COMPANY:
COMING FROM:
GOING TO:
OTHER INFORMATION:

| DATE: |
| TIME: |
| TRAIN: |
| |
| HEADCODE: |
| OPERATING COMPANY: |
| |
| COMING FROM: |
| |
| GOING TO: |
| |
| OTHER INFORMATION: |
| |
| |
| |
| |
| |
| |
| |
| |
| |

DATE:
TIME:
TRAIN:
HEADCODE:
OPERATING COMPANY:
COMING FROM:
GOING TO:
OTHER INFORMATION:

DATE:
TIME:
TRAIN:
HEADCODE:
OPERATING COMPANY:
COMING FROM:
GOING TO:
OTHER INFORMATION:

DATE:
TIME:
TRAIN:
HEADCODE:
OPERATING COMPANY:
COMING FROM:
GOING TO:
OTHER INFORMATION:

DATE:
TIME:
TRAIN:
HEADCODE:
OPERATING COMPANY:
COMING FROM:
GOING TO:
OTHER INFORMATION:

DATE:	
TIME:	
TRAIN:	
HEADCODE:	
OPERATING COMPANY:	
COMING FROM:	
GOING TO:	
OTHER INFORMATION:	

DATE:
TIME:
TRAIN:
HEADCODE:
OPERATING COMPANY:
COMING FROM:
GOING TO:
OTHER INFORMATION:

DATE:
TIME:
TRAIN:
HEADCODE:
OPERATING COMPANY:
COMING FROM:
GOING TO:
OTHER INFORMATION:

DATE:
TIME:
TRAIN:
HEADCODE:
OPERATING COMPANY:
COMING FROM:
GOING TO:
OTHER INFORMATION:

DATE:
TIME:
TRAIN:
HEADCODE:
OPERATING COMPANY:
COMING FROM:
GOING TO:
OTHER INFORMATION:

| DATE: |
| TIME: |
| TRAIN: |
| |
| HEADCODE: |
| OPERATING COMPANY: |
| |
| COMING FROM: |
| |
| GOING TO: |
| |
| OTHER INFORMATION: |
| |
| |
| |
| |
| |
| |
| |
| |
| |
| |

DATE:
TIME:
TRAIN:
HEADCODE:
OPERATING COMPANY:
COMING FROM:
GOING TO:
OTHER INFORMATION:

DATE:
TIME:
TRAIN:
HEADCODE:
OPERATING COMPANY:
COMING FROM:
GOING TO:
OTHER INFORMATION:

DATE:
TIME:
TRAIN:
HEADCODE:
OPERATING COMPANY:
COMING FROM:
GOING TO:
OTHER INFORMATION:

DATE:
TIME:
TRAIN:
HEADCODE:
OPERATING COMPANY:
COMING FROM:
GOING TO:
OTHER INFORMATION:

DATE:
TIME:
TRAIN:
HEADCODE:
OPERATING COMPANY:
COMING FROM:
GOING TO:
OTHER INFORMATION:

| DATE: |
| TIME: |
| TRAIN: |
| |
| HEADCODE: |
| OPERATING COMPANY: |
| |
| COMING FROM: |
| |
| GOING TO: |
| |
| OTHER INFORMATION: |
| |
| |
| |
| |
| |
| |
| |
| |
| |
| |

DATE:
TIME:
TRAIN:
HEADCODE:
OPERATING COMPANY:
COMING FROM:
GOING TO:
OTHER INFORMATION:

DATE:
TIME:
TRAIN:
HEADCODE:
OPERATING COMPANY:
COMING FROM:
GOING TO:
OTHER INFORMATION:

FINALLY...

I really hope you've enjoyed using this notebook as much as I enjoyed making it.

Toodle-pip!

Printed in Great Britain
by Amazon